I'm a Grandparent!
Now What Do I Do?

By Roger and Dottie Small

SCHOOLHOUSE PUBLISHING
659 Schoolhouse Road
Telford, PA 18969
www.shpublishing.com

I'm a Grandparent! Now What Do I Do?

Copyright © 2008 by Roger and Dottie Small

Published by   Schoolhouse Publishing
                   659 Schoolhouse Road
                   Telford, PA 18969
                   www.shpublishing.com

Cover design and original artwork: Seth Aaron Jones

Seth Aaron Jones can be contacted through Schoolhouse Publishing.

First Printing, 2008

Printed in the United States of America

DEDICATION

"Unless the Lord builds the house, those who built it labor in vain." Psalm 127:1 ESV

We would like to dedicate this book…
…to our *Heavenly Father* for His grace and mercy,
…to *Jesus Christ* our Savior and Lord,
…and to the *Holy Spirit* for enabling us to write this book,

AND

…to our three daughters, Kim, Robin, Lisa, and their husbands, who have blessed us with our thirteen grandchildren and our first great grandchild.

ACKNOWLEDGMENTS

We want to express our deep gratitude for the sacrificial labor of love to the following dear brothers and sisters who have made this book a reality.

Aron Osborne and the pastoral staff - for their prayers and support to keep going...

Warren Boettcher - for initiating this project, encouraging us to write the book...

Kim Boettcher - for encouraging us to complete the book and for editing and typing the manuscript...

Troy Mart - for the many hours spent editing the book...

Seth Jones - for his outstanding art work on the cover and throughout the book...

Robin Witter, Lisa Blankenship, Denise Randolph, Sheri Hughes, Toni Sharp - for their faithfulness to read the manuscript...

Dale and Susie Kemmerer - for the final editing and publishing of the book.

Table of Contents

Forward

"One generation shall commend your works to another, and shall declare your mighty acts...They shall speak of the might of your awesome deeds, and I will declare your greatness. They shall pour forth the fame of your abundant goodness and shall sing aloud of your righteousness."

Psalm 145:4, 6-7 ESV

This wonderful charge is given to those who know Jesus Christ as their Savior to tell the next generation about His greatness and grace. I have had the privilege to know Roger and Dottie Small for more than 35 years - the last 28 years as their son-in-law - and they have and are fulfilling this great commission. I am personally experiencing the wonderful fruit of their parenting by enjoying marriage with their oldest daughter Kim (the most godly and beautiful woman I can imagine) and have seen them up close and personal as grandparents to our children. Not only have they excelled as parents to their three daughters and as in-laws to their three sons-in-law, but they have also been excellent grandparents to all thirteen of their grandchildren and their one great-grandchild. Their lives 'sing aloud' of the goodness and faithfulness of God to our family.

This is a couple that has lived to serve the next generation. They have done that with their time, energy, and resources. They have consistently postured themselves to support us because in their own words, "it is our children's time now" as we are the ones doing the "more important work." They have been selfless in how they have lived out this season of their lives. Rather than come across as 'experts,' they have specifically encouraged us in our parenting as well as in our marriages. Because of the testimony of their genuine humility, it has only led us (the next generation) to want to relate to them and learn from

3

them even more. Their godly character, love for the Savior and the church, and their desire to put our interests above their own have modeled Christ's heart to serve and has left their children and grandchildren with a wonderful Christian legacy and powerful example to follow. You have in your hands some of the fruit of their labors. While you may not be able to imitate all they have done, with the same help of God's grace that they have experienced, you can certainly imitate their hearts. Mom and Dad, on behalf of your girls, your son-in-laws, and your grandchildren, thank you for your example and for modeling Christ-exalting godliness to multiple generations. We love you!

Warren Boettcher
Senior Pastor, Sovereign Grace Church

Introduction

As the daylight slowly appeared under the dark window shades in our bedroom, we were startled by the ring of the telephone. Groping in the dark beside the bed, half asleep, I answered.

"It's a girl!" my son–in–law's voice excitedly announced. Our first grandchild had arrived: 7 pounds, 2 ounces and 19 inches long. Her cry was long and loud; there was no problem with her lungs! Mom was doing well, recovering in her room. What good news!

For the past nine months we had been waiting for this call. Our oldest daughter was now a mother, which was a mental adjustment of its own. I (Dottie) remember the first time I saw her in the hospital after she delivered her baby. She looked totally drained. With tears in my eyes, I thought to myself, "You labored so hard to give me this beautiful grandchild." It was very humbling to see my daughter lying there exhausted. I couldn't do anything to help her except to rejoice with her. She had done all the work. We were grandparents. Now what do we do?

5

After the seemingly never-ending years of diapers, whining babies, disciplining, teaching, counseling, the 'car keys,' and weddings, we had to ask ourselves the question: *Were we ready to be grandparents?* There was always the temptation to buy a new car, to travel abroad, to build a new home, or to take a cruise. Why not? After all, our parenting days were over.

However, that afternoon our whole mindset changed when we got a first glimpse of our granddaughter through the nursery window cuddled in a pink blanket. Somehow a new car, traveling abroad, building a new house, or taking a cruise fell far short compared to God's gift we held in our arms. The Lord had breathed new life into our family, and we knew then that we wanted to play an active part in our granddaughter's life.

As we have contemplated writing this book, we have prayed that our story would in some way touch the heart of young grandparents. In today's culture it is very difficult to raise a Christian family. We are like salmon swimming upstream in a strong current. The culture says that it takes a village to raise a child. Instead, we prefer to believe that the Lord has established the family with a mom and a dad to raise a child, and grandparents play a significant role in assisting them.

A healthy gospel-believing local church also plays a very important role in a child's life. The pastoral influence should both encourage and demonstrate. They should teach the fathers to lead in the home and to love their wives as Christ loves the church. They should teach the women to respect their husbands by submitting to them as unto the Lord. These contribute to a peaceable home environment for the Lord to be honored and for the children to mature.

It is our desire to share the lessons that we have learned. We hope to bring some encouragement and vision to the next generation of grandparents. If you are reading this book, and you are a Christian grandparent, be encouraged. The Lord will guide you and enable you to do what He's called you to do. What He has done for us, He will do for you. It may look differently, but the principles and His grace will be the same. His grace is more than sufficient to enable us to grandparent in a way that honors Him and blesses our children and our grandchildren.

What Legacy Will We Leave?

"So even to old age and gray hairs, O God, do not forsake me, until I proclaim your might to another generation, your power to all those to come."

Psalm 71:18 ESV

"The righteous flourish like the palm tree and grow like a cedar in Lebanon. They are planted in the house of the Lord; they flourish in the courts of our God. They still bear fruit in old age; they are ever full of sap and green, to declare that the LORD is upright; he is my rock, and there is no unrighteousness in him."

Psalm 92:12-15 ESV

July 2, 1983, added a new dimension to our lives. Our first grandchild was born, and we now faced many new challenging questions:

- What role did we now have in the family?
- Where did we fit in?
- What is God now calling us to do in helping to fulfill His plan for our family?

The days in which grandparents owned the family farm and the sons and daughters worked and waited to inherit are long gone. Today many children not only live far away, but also earn more money than their own parents. Therefore, the financial dependency of grown children on their parents no longer exists. Furthermore, distance often makes contact with grandchildren to be intermittent at best. So, is there a place for grandparents in the nurturing of grandchildren in this generation? If so, what is our place?

We had further questions:

- What kind of legacy did we want to leave to our grandchildren?
- What kind of impact could we have on their lives?
- Did our lives really matter to them?

We realized we needed to go to God's Word for some answers. In Jeremiah 35 we found a very amazing story about the effects of a father's wisdom passed on to his children. It is the story of the obedience of the Rechabites. Jonadab, a Rechabite, was not an Israelite. He and his family lived among the children of Israel. When Jonadab died he left a legacy to his sons which later influenced at least twelve subsequent generations. His family lived in safety and good health during those generations. They had such high respect for their father's wisdom that they passed it on down for twelve generations. Jonadab advised his sons and grandsons to not drink wine, build houses nor plant fields to grow a vineyard. Instead, they became nomads living in tents, and raised sheep for many generations.

By not raising crops their lifestyle did not interfere with the lives of the Jews among whom they lived. As Jonadab had foreseen, they were able to live peaceably in the land. The legacy of not drinking wine evidently bore great fruit in sustaining the high moral character of the family, which was a delight to God. When the King of Babylon came up against their land, the Rechabites found it necessary to take refuge in Jerusalem. The Lord was pleased with their obedience to their father's legacy and very disappointed with the disobedience of His own people (Jeremiah 35:18, 19).

In bitter contrast is the account of King Saul whose unjust persecution of the Gibeonites, in violation of the promise that Joshua had made to them, resulted in the death of two of his sons and five of his grandsons (2 Samuel 21:8, 9). Obviously, King Saul did not consider how his actions would affect his offspring.

Exodus 34:6, 7 (ESV) says, *"The LORD, the LORD, a God merciful and gracious, slow to anger, and abounding in steadfast love and faithfulness, keeping steadfast love for thousands, forgiving iniquity and transgression and sin, but who will by no means clear the guilty, visiting the iniquity of the fathers on the children and the children's children, to the third and fourth generation."* As grandparents, we affect the next generation. We do matter. With age comes wisdom, godly wisdom. Realizing we needed wisdom, we have asked the Lord for it continually - and for lots of it!

In this book we share our testimony of God's enabling grace as well as a number of insights that we have discovered along the way. We have been grandparenting for 25 years and are still learning the value of our relationship with the Lord. We are continuing to develop a deeper friendship with our own children and a more inclusive relationship with the in-laws. By strengthening these relationships, we have been blessed to grow more intimate with our grandchildren. God's word says, *"Children are a heritage from the Lord"* (Psalm 127:3 ESV). Indeed they are, and grandchildren are a double portion of that blessing.

We have just entered a new season of great-grandparenting, and now more than ever we are asking ourselves *what kind of legacy do we want to leave to our* grandchildren and great grandchildren to build upon? We could continue to buy them gifts, take them new places, and build special memories with them, which in itself is a rich legacy. However, as we have pondered this thought, we believe that the greatest legacy we can leave with our grandchildren and great grandchildren is to point them to the Lord Jesus Christ.   They need Jesus more than anything we could ever do or buy for them. It is God alone who calls them and reveals their need to repent and to be born again. We now have an opportunity to influence, encourage, and pray our grandchildren toward eternity.

"So shall my Word be that goes out from my mouth; it shall not return to me empty, but it shall accomplish that which I purpose, and shall succeed in the thing for which I sent it."
Isaiah 55:11 ESV

Who Am I?

"For I know the plans I have for you, declares the LORD, plans for wholeness and not for evil, to give you a future and a hope."   Jeremiah 29:11 ESV

"Blessed be the God and Father of our Lord Jesus Christ, who has blessed us in Christ with every spiritual blessing in the heavenly places, even as he chose us in him before the foundation of the world, that we should be holy and blameless before him. In love he predestined us for adoption through Jesus Christ, according to the purpose of his will, to the praise of his glorious grace, with which he has blessed us in the Beloved."   Ephesians 1:3-6 ESV

Who am I? Where did I come from? Why am I here? These are familiar questions that we all have asked. There was a time in my (Roger's) life when I would have loved to have had a grandparent to tell me stories about my mother and father and where they grew up.

I was three years old when my mother died, and it was a very traumatic event for me. Because my father was in the 13 military during World War II, my mother and I lived a great distance away from the rest of the family. Thus, my mother was my only real relationship in the world. When she died, everyone at the funeral was a stranger to me and my connection to the world was gone. Due to circumstances and adding to my confusion, my baby sister and I did not go to live with any member of the family. Basically, we lived in several elder care boarding houses while our father was away at sea. It was also thought best that no mention ever be made of our mother by anyone. Even my toys were taken from me, hoping to remove any memory of that upsetting time in my life. Thus, I grew up completely bewildered and very vulnerable to peer pressure. I did not have anyone telling me who I was and why I was born.

The world became a battleground of defining my identity. Each group and individual that I met would often provoke feelings of hatred, superiority or inferiority. I had no idea that I was responding to my sinful nature. I was lost in a world of darkness, wandering around blindfolded and unable to obey God's commandment to love one another. I was consumed with my own importance and desire for love and acceptance.

On the other hand, Dottie's identity was so different growing up. She was raised in a big farm family who encouraged her in many ways. Growing up in a religious environment, she attended Sunday school and even taught a few classes. She thought she had it all together until the age of 31 when she discovered that she really didn't know who she was either. God was working in her heart as she began to ask questions about her existence and why she was here. She was tired of giving thanks and praying to someone she didn't know. If God was alive, she wanted to personally know Him.

It was shortly after she started asking these questions that she heard the gospel for the first time. As good a person as she tried to be and believed herself to be, she heard that she was a sinner and needed a Savior. When Dottie repented and received Jesus, you would have thought she was the last Gentile saved! The change was so dramatic. Thankfully, the Lord convicted me (Roger) soon after, and I also was born again. Our three daughters followed a few years later.

Knowing the truth that Dottie and I were born sinners in need of a Savior has truly helped us as grandparents to be patient with our grandchildren's sinful behavior and to pray for their salvation. Until they come to realize that Jesus died for their sins, we continue to stand in the gap, praying for conviction of sin, the gift of repentance, faith towards God, and the revelation that they must be born again. In the meantime we are blessed to love them, enjoy them, and reveal Jesus to them through our behavior.

To be honest, there have been times when we have grown impatient with a grandchild and allowed our speech to express it. We have come to realize how important it is to acknowledge our impatient tone of voice as sin and ask them to forgive us for speaking unkindly. Grandchildren have a very high expectation of their grandparents' behavior and they need to see that we also answer to Jesus.

Building Blocks of a Legacy

As the grandchildren were growing up, there was something we didn't realize at the time. We, along with their parents, were instilling in them a confidence as to who God had created them to be. We each loved affirming their God-given gifts and talents, and we also enjoyed pointing out to them the changes that God was making in their character. For example on their birthdays, we would write in their cards something to let them know that we loved them and saw Jesus at work in their lives. For instance, it might be something like these:

- "You have such a tender heart."
- "We love the way you care for your pets."
- "The Lord has blessed you with a gift of music."
- "We are glad that God created you for us to love."

Legacy Stories Passed Down

Throughout our their childhood, we liked to tell our grandchildren stories that were handed down to us. For example we'd share, "Did you know that your great, great grandfather was supposed to take a ferry boat ride from Portland, Maine, to Peaks Island? He was too late and missed his ride. That night the ferry boat sank and many died. His life was spared. Just think about it. If he had died, where would you be?" This story would open a whole new discussion about life and how we were related to one another as family.

Another story we would share is about their great grandfather during World War II and how the Lord spared his life. One night many ships in his convoy were sunk, but his ship was saved. Both of these stories gave us an opportunity to share the sovereignty of God in our lives and the protection of His plan for man.

Legacy Vacation

When the grandchildren were around nine years old, we began to take them individually on trips to New England with us. We grew up in that area and still have that New England accent! Our destination was our family camp nestled

in the pine trees with plenty of hiking trails on the shores of a lake in New Hampshire. Each summer we would spend a week there with Dottie's folks. Our first stop on the way was Connecticut to visit Great, Great Grandma Robinson who was living in a nursing home. To capture the moment, we had our video camera in hand. We encouraged the grandchildren to ask her all kinds of questions:

- "Where did you grow up?"
- "How old are you?"
- "What was school like in a one room school house?"
- "Did you have a television when you grew up?"
- "Who did you marry?"
- "Did you know Jesus?"

Unfortunately, only our three oldest grandchildren were able to spend time with their great, great grandmother before she went home to be with the Lord at the age of 101 years.

The next stop was Dottie's hometown in Massachusetts. Dottie was raised on a farm that had been in the family for four generations. Imagine her thrill as a grandmother to show the grandchildren through the town in which she grew up. We viewed the school she attended through high school, the church where we were married, and for special fun, we'd take the grandchildren past the house where we raised their mother and aunts. The trip through town would end up with a huge banana split at the ice cream store where Dottie worked 50 years earlier to earn money for college. At the end of the day we would arrive at camp exhausted but ready for new adventures.

Legacy Photos

Another idea that the Lord gave us to help our grandchildren feel loved and accepted was to create a wall of photographs in our kitchen that features each of our grandchildren. We have been amazed how many times a

grandchild has come in to the kitchen and made some comment about his or her picture. Arranged in families, the mothers have kept us up to date with their latest pictures. When our first grandchild was married, we put her wedding picture in the place of her senior picture. Later, when she had her first child, we put our great granddaughter's picture above her daddy and mommy. More recent pictures are displayed on the refrigerator. This display changes more frequently.

We also have individual photo albums featuring each of our grandchildren, documenting milestones of their lives. Along with these photo albums, we have tucked their little letters to us written in their youthful handwriting. As our grandchildren look at their albums together with their cousins, we often hear them giggling and laughing as they recall the events surrounding each picture.

Speaking of pictures, the grandchildren love to learn about their heritage by looking at old heirloom family photos. On the wall going upstairs, we have arranged pictures of the generations that also include the newest generations. In fact, the oldest photo on the wall is about 120 years old. Each one of these pictures has a story to tell. Our grandchildren love to hear them all. We even have a picture of me standing with my mother and father. This picture has given opportunity to share how my mother died, where I went to live, and how God cared for me during that time in my life. We always ends with our wedding photos and our love story which the children love to hear again and again.

Most amazing to us has been how these pictures have helped our precious little ten year old granddaughter from China. Positioned right there among the whole family, her

photo declares that she is one of us. When she was 14 months old, her parents brought her home from China. She knows that she is adopted. Her mommy and daddy tell her 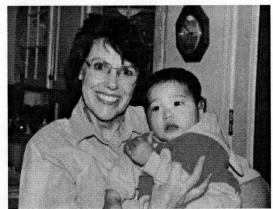 that though she has birth parents in China, they carried her in their hearts long before she was born. When she is older she will understand more, but for now she knows she is family and that is enough.

We trust that the time we spend with our grandchildren passing on to them the stories told to us, will continue to give them a stronger sense of God's divine plan for who they are, where they came from, and why they are here. As they grow in their faith, they will come to understand their greatest purpose in this life is to glorify God by enjoying Him forever.

3

Relating to and Serving Our Children

"Train up a child in the way he should go; even when he is old he will not depart from it."   Proverb 22:6 ESV

"But if we walk in the light, as he is in the light, we have fellowship with one another, and the blood of Jesus his Son cleanses us from all sin."   I John 1:7 ESV

"But whoever would be great among you must be your servant, and whoever would be first among you must be your slave, even as the Son of Man came not to be served but to serve, and to give his life as a ransom for many."
        Matthew 20:26-28 ESV

When we first became grandparents, the sinful attitudes of, *'We know, been there, done that,'* were all present. It was a struggle to let the young parents learn for themselves and for us to support their ideas. Our tendency to be judgmental did not help us to have healthy, godly relationships with our daughters and sons-in-law. Our own pride and self-serving attitudes made it difficult to relate. We thought our ideas should be considered. Instead, we needed to learn how to serve our children in their new roles, not control their lives. We had to learn to step back and encourage our children as they cared for their families. They were a couple, a family, a team. Coming alongside of them, sometimes with a meal, or babysitting, or a word of encouragement or prayer was what they needed. However, we wanted to be asked.

There was a problem with 'wanting to be asked.' Our relationship with our married children was still developing. We thought that we were doing the right thing by sitting back and waiting to be asked. However, the couple with the new baby wanted us to *volunteer* to help. It was awkward for them to ask for help, but we thought it was imposing on our part to offer assistance. Once we realized our presumption about each other, it brought a better understanding and improved our relationship.

Our relationship with our children is very sanctifying. To be able to *speak the truth in love* isn't natural. We are still learning. Speaking the truth in love does open the door many times to deeper conversations. However, there are times when it is just better to be quiet. In the movie *Bambi*, Thumper's mother said it best: "If you can't say anything nice, don't say anything at all." More importantly, scripture exhorts us, "*Let no corrupting talk come out of your mouths, but only such as is good for building up, as fits the occasion, that it may give grace to those who hear*" (Ephesians 4:29 ESV).

We found that expressing critical words will quickly shut down conversation. This is especially true when that grandbaby arrives. We had to constantly remind ourselves that *they are the parents and we are the grandparents*. They need our prayers, respect and support as they begin their new responsibility, not our judgment.

It is a blessing to serve the family and watch the generations emerge. We are now in a position to be available to serve our children in a new way. But, we had to learn this.

Realizing we were not stepping down from our responsibility as parents when we became grandparents but simply refashioning our role, helped us immensely in the transition. Our daughters were now married and starting their own families. The question we now ask ourselves is *how can we best serve them and their families without crossing boundaries?* Our relationship was changing, but we soon realized how mutually beneficial our relationship would be for the grandchildren as well.

As our relationship with the girls and their spouses has grown over the years, we are realizing that we are not only their friends to enjoy an evening of discussion, dinner and games, but also servants looking for ways to support them in their role as parents. Being available for prayer, advice, counsel, or physical help is crucial.

There are so many ways we have learned to serve our children. One way has been by fitting into our children's plans rather than having a rigid schedule of our own. By being flexible with our plans, we reduce the stress on the families of our children. This flexibility is essential in regard to holidays and vacation times. It is difficult with the many families' activities to find a day or week that is right for everyone. We have to remind ourselves that *they are the main event.* We allow the younger families to make initial plans and we generally conform to their decision.

Sharing the burden of the family dinner is one way we help each other. Dottie will usually provide the meat and one vegetable dish. The girls all fill in with the rest of the meal. In fact, even our married granddaughter Julie adds a new dimension. Her mother let Julie experiment in the kitchen while she was still a young teenager. She loved to bake cookies for the family. And now, she is a great cook though she is just a newlywed.

Praying is another way we have tried to support our children's families. There have been times when our daughters will call and just say, "*Pray!*" Details are not important; it is a family matter. If they wished to talk about it, we were ready to listen. This is especially important when the grandchildren are teenagers. They do not want us to know anything that they might be doing wrong. Sooner or later a grandchild may tell us about a situation in his or her own way. We have tried not to let the grandchildren think that Mom and Dad tell us everything, because they don't. It is enough comfort for us to remember that the Lord is praying continually for them and working out the details. His plan for each family is His own.

We also try to keep in mind that we are the grandparents, not the parents. We have found that this gives us the freedom to make suggestions or observations, but the decision is always theirs to make. It is helpful to learn their ideas about parenting so that we can support them. For instance, when we are babysitting we like to know what the parents expect. Often the parents will leave instructions to follow: bedtime, no candy, one story, one small glass of water, no juice, etc. Being mindful of their instructions gives the parents a peace of mind and also ensures them that our grandchildren know that we honor their parents. We will report any discipline problem. We use 'time out' in a special chair or speak in a firm voice (not yelling), and they know we mean it. The grandchildren understand that they will be disciplined later by Mommy and Daddy if necessary. As grandparents, it helps us to know that their parents are following through with discipline. Sharing with their parents any bad attitudes or disrespect we might encounter is helping to build our grandchildren's character in some small way.

Another way we seek to serve the girls is to make sure that they give the larger gift to our grandchild at Christmas or a birthday. If the parents cannot afford it, we like to quietly help. As a result, we ensure that the grandchildren continue to look to their parents rather than us as the primary gift givers. As a rule, we do not give expensive gifts. Anyway, having thirteen grandchildren makes that an impossibility! Asking the grandchildren for their Christmas lists enables us to get them something they really like. Usually the older teens like gift cards or money. For the younger children we have fun shopping at the toy store.

One of our greatest challenges was to stay in touch with our youngest daughter's family when she lived three hours from us. It was especially hard to adjust because we are a very close family and love to be together. Even our sons-in-law are like sons to us and all of the grandchildren share a very close cousin relationship. We miss each other when we cannot be together.

Long-distance grandparenting can have its advantages. For instance, we found that we use the phone more. Every Sunday at nine, Lisa would call and we would talk until we had nothing more to say. Cell phones are great! The grandchildren would get on the phone and would talk about what they were doing in school, at work, in sports and with their pets.

Friends of ours have made it a practice of sending videos back and forth to their grandchildren. What a great idea. After a while, they will have a whole library of the lives of their grandchildren.

When Doug and Lisa had the opportunity for a getaway weekend, we loved to drive down and care for their children. Opportunities to play games, to watch videos, to play in the park, to take hikes, to make trips to the dollar store, and  to tell plenty of made-up stories, made it a memorable time. Since the children were homeschooled, we were able to help them with any difficult areas in their schooling while we were there.

Speaking of homeschooling, that was a whole new concept of education for us. Public school and Christian school worked for us. What was this homeschooling all about? Again, we were full of questions: *Was it legal? What had changed their mind? How would it affect them socially? Could they teach competently?* As young grandparents, it took us a while to adjust to the idea. It was obvious that the parents had diligently researched and prayed it through; it was not just a quick idea they simply wanted to try. They were very gracious and patient with us as we tried to understand this new idea of schooling.

By the time our oldest grandchild was in third grade, her test results were very acceptable. Our daughter, Kim, had taught her to read, write, add, subtract, and other subjects as well. Soon following she started our next grandchild in first grade. Through expanding the capacities of our daughter in teaching her children, God was blessing this family.

Looking back, we now realize we could have helped much more with the housework, ironing, making a meal, taking the younger children to the park, reading to the children or having them read to us - simply anything to relieve Mom. She had dedicated her life to teaching our grandchildren and it was more than a full-time job.

Today homeschooling is well accepted and has proven its merits. However, we have come to understand that homeschooling is not for everyone. It is a very prayerful, year-by-year, decision for each family. The grandchildren's education is important to us and we realize more than ever the value of our prayers.

In our family the Lord has enabled us to successfully experience homeschool, Christian school and public school education - each having its own merits. The parents have been able to discern through prayer the appropriate education for each one of our grandchildren.

While we have looked for ways to serve our adult children, they have served us in sound counsel. For instance, when Roger found a job in the same community as one of our daughters, we had to make a major move. Additionally, Dottie's folks were elderly and needed personal care, so we decided to purchase a new home with an in-law suite. All three daughters and their husbands were great counselors to us as we thought through the process of moving. All the daughters strongly opposed moving into an adult community. Knowing how much we enjoy all kinds of folks, they thought being surrounded by people only our age would limit us. They were right. An adult community would have inhibited our family lifestyle at this stage of our life; plus it would have prevented our home from being used in a church-plant situation.

Another daughter suggested we consider acquiring a home near her so she would be able to help with her grandmother and grandfather. With her growing family and our need, we decided to build a new home seven minutes from her. While the home was under construction, Mike and Robin graciously took us in for five months. Our grandson Ben gave up his room and he and Matthew bunked together in a much smaller room. It is one of our most precious memories with Robin's family. Moving to this area has allowed us to live the nearest we have ever been to any of our adult children. Among the many blessings of living nearby is being able to baby sit on short notice. For the seven years while Dottie's parents were living with us, Robin was always graciously available to step in and relieve Dottie when she needed help or just a break.

As we sit on the edge of another generation, a new door has opened. We have become great grandparents. This has brought a new and delightful challenge into our lives. We now must in effect take another 'step back' to leave room for our children themselves to be grandparents.

I (Dottie) was first made aware of this reality when I was out shopping for a baby shower gift. As I made my way to the checkout counter, I spotted a clearance sale of darling little girl dresses. Without thinking I found the cutest little three-piece outfit: coat, dress, and hat. It was half price and a I immediately thought of my great granddaughter for Easter. I picked it off the rack, put it in my shopping cart, and started for the checkout.

On my way there this thought came to my mind, "*You are not the grandmother or the mother. You had better first ask your granddaughter and your daughter to see what their plans are before you just make an assumption and buy an outfit.*" I knew then that it had to be the Lord reminding me not take away my daughter's delight in providing an Easter outfit for her first granddaughter. As a grandmother it was my honor when the grandchildren were small to sew Easter outfits for them - shirts and pants for the little boys and dresses for the little girls. I loved it.

In an e-mail when I asked my granddaughter and daughter what their plans were, I was so grateful that I listened to that 'still small voice' whispering in my ear. My granddaughter already had an outfit she wanted Mackenzie to wear, and my daughter had purchased Mackenzie a new spring everyday outfit as well. In that same e-mail my granddaughter suggested that I start a new 'great-grandmother tradition' by buying one of the accessories, like a pair of shoes, a pocketbook, or hat, etc. What a great idea!

We have become aware that it is now our time to take another step back and draw closer to the Lord. We desire to always remember that Mommy and Daddy are now the main event, and Grandma and Grandpa come before Great-Grandma and Great-Grandpa. Our grandchildren will be raising the next generation and our prayers for them need to be heard. The Lord is listening and He will meet their need and our need as well. The journey to our eternal home continues.

Our Relationship With the In-Laws

"Love covers a multitude of sin."   I Peter 4:8 ESV

"One generation shall commend your works to another, and shall declare your mighty acts."
                                                      Psalm 145:4 ESV

     With our noses pressing up against the nursery window and our eyes beholding the most beautiful baby in the world, we shared similar thoughts...
     "My son's baby..."
     "My daughter's baby..."
     "My grandchild!"
...Turning to each other we cry and hug. We're so proud of our children. Grandparenting is now a reality. Sharing our grandparenting with in-laws is the journey before us.
     Every first time grandparent has his or her own story. For us, it felt like we were now ready to be parents! Strange as that may seem, our years of parenting in some ways were like an

experiment. We were young without much teaching, and learned from our mistakes along the way. Fortunately, by the time we were grandparents, we were growing in the Word of God and being trained by it.

We soon found out that grandparenting had its own lessons to be learned and that we did not have all the answers. It wasn't long before we realized that we were not the only grandparents in our granddaughter's life. There was another grandmother, a very dear, godly lady who was twenty years our senior. Ruth, affectionately called Nana, was already an excellent grandmother and had just lost her dear husband, Andy. Additionally, she shared a very close relationship with our daughter, which we greatly appreciated- that is until the birth of our granddaughter.

I felt threatened and immature. The alienating sin of jealousy started to creep into my friendship with Ruth. Being replaced by another grandmother was overwhelming to me emotionally. The thought that my granddaughter would love Nana more gripped my heart.

Thankfully, the kindness of God broke in and exposed my spirit of competition. Very simply, I wanted to be the favorite grandmother. Pride ruled my heart. Lacking confidence to develop my own relationship with my new granddaughter, I didn't know where to start. Sadly, fear began to interfere with my relationship with my daughter. Kim felt caught in the middle between two doting grandmothers.

To this day, I am thankful for the strong conviction and determination that the Lord placed within my heart to not agree with that sin of jealousy. I needed to repent. God's kindness led me to repentance, and He opened my eyes to see what was most important: a God-honoring relationship with Ruth. My relationship with my granddaughter Julie would develop in time. In fact, I could *observe* Ruth and *learn* from her experience.

A few years later when our oldest granddaughter was three, we all went out for dinner. When we arrived at the restaurant, Julie asked me if we could sit together. "After all," Julie said as she tossed her hair, "adults are so boring!" I had to chuckle; we were developing our own relationship.

As parents of three daughters, we tried to impress upon the girls the importance of developing a personal relationship with their in-laws. We felt that it was important for our grandchildren to know that their Daddy's parents loved them too. Our girls have done a great job at reaching out to their in-laws and including them in family activities.

There is a saying, "A son is a son until he takes a wife, but a daughter is a daughter for the rest of her life." Although that saying may sound cute, it can also be painful in a family where *leaving and cleaving* is not clearly understood. The following story is true. It happened to our good friends. They wanted us to share their story to perhaps prevent this same situation from happening in another extended family relationship.

Karen (not her real name) begins the story: "Both of our families were extremely delighted about the prospect of our children's marriage. Our children had known each other from childhood. It would be a glorious event and a great celebration. Our two families were so happy - until that glorious/fateful day when our first grandchild was born. Then, overnight, it was like everything changed. The bond between our two families was ripped apart. Our hearts were broken. Where did we go wrong?

Once the baby came, it was obvious that our daughter-in-law only wanted her mother. We felt rejected. After all, this was our grandchild too! Sadly, we chose to withdraw and missed the early days of our grandson's life.

By the time our second grandchild was born, we had learned a most valuable lesson: *we were not rejected.* Understanding that special bond between a mother and her daughter brought healing to our relationship. Our failure with the first grandbaby had driven a wedge between our two families and we didn't want this to happen again. Wanting one's mother is normal for a daughter during that season of life as she adjusts to her new role. We had to learn to step back, to not push ourselves on our daughter-in-law, and to give her hormones time to readjust.

We also realized we had not prepared our own son to lead his wife through this trial. Between two strongly-opinionated grandmothers, he was getting overwhelmed emotionally and finding it difficult to be in control of his own home. His father and father-in-law fell short by not giving him the support and encouragement he needed to take responsibility in his own home. We can only pray we have learned something to pass on to others."

We really appreciate the humility of our friends in sharing this story. It demonstrates the importance of being teachable and willing to learn from mistakes. Being strongly opinionated separates families. Romans 14:15 reminds us to pursue things that make for peace. Pursuing things that make for peace helps to keep the harmony in the family for the sake of the grandchildren; but most importantly, it honors the Lord.

Our relationship with the in-laws has continued to grow over the years. We give our daughters the credit for this. They have been faithful to include us in various family celebrations. For instance, our daughter living nearby has made it her practice to invite both sets of grandparents to birthday parties for the children. Since we both live in the same area, it

Baby Ben with both sets of grandparents - the Witters and the Smalls.

is very kind of her to consider us. We don't always see her in-laws on a regular basis, so having dinner together is very special. It demonstrates a value that both sets of grandparents are treasured. For years we have exchanged Christmas gifts with the in-laws, even the ones who live far away. We like to remember and always thank them for raising our sons-in-law. We have encouraged our daughters to consider their in-laws before us, especially for holidays. As an extended family, it is often easier for us to celebrate at a later time when we can all still be together.

Our sons-in-law call us "mom" and "dad". We love it. Graciously God provided three incredible sons to love and provide for our daughters. We can only praise the Lord for the parents of those boys. That is why we believe it important to encourage our own daughters to nurture the relationship with their in-laws. Each of these women raised her son to be the husband he is today. Each has also learned to release her son to another woman, her daughter-in-law, to love. In a sense, our daughters received the fruit of their labors!

In the past 24 years with three daughters married, it has been a challenge to remember that there is another set of grandparents that love our grandchildren just as much as we do. By the grace of God, we have grown to appreciate their healthy influence with our grandchildren. The in-laws have certainly played an equally-important role in supporting and strengthening the family. The grandchildren have benefited greatly from having two sets of grandparents. We are most grateful to be one of those sets of grandparents.

In this culture where divorce and remarriage is so prevalent, we admire the married couples who have done an excellent job of honoring their parents. Often with four sets of grandparents, their holidays and special visits become a real challenge. It is not easy. We have some friends who are the same age as our children who are excellent examples of this difficult circumstance. We have witnessed their unwavering devotion to each side of the family and the major affect that it has had on their children. Their friendship with each of their parents has made the children feel very confident and special. In their commitment to honor their parents, the Lord has blessed them many times. They have been able to work out birthdays, holidays, and other visits, so that the children are able to continue building a relationship with their grandparents. We greatly admire this couple's desire to honor their parents as unto the Lord, as God still honors obedience to the fifth commandment: *"Honor your father and mother, that your days may be long in the land that the LORD your God is giving you." (Exodus 20:12 ESV)*

Two sets of grandparents enjoying a day together: the Blankenships and the Smalls.

Building a Relationship With our Grandchildren

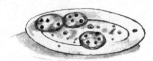

"The steadfast love of the Lord is from everlasting to everlasting on those who fear him, and his righteousness to children's children, to those who keep his covenant and remember to do his commandments."   *Psalm 103:17, 18 ESV*

There is a bumper sticker that says something like, "If I knew that grandparenting would be so much fun I'd have had my grandchildren first." This is true in so many ways.   Now after 25 years of parenting, God has graciously rewarded us with our 13 grandchildren and they are FUN! They came into our lives like little stepping stones: They are Julie (24), Ben (23), Jeff (22), Matt (21), Amy (20), Kristie (18), Andy (17), Kevin (15), Grant (14), Timothy (11), Melanie (10), Stephen (10) and ending with Lianna (9). We treasure each one. We could write a book about each grandchild and never finish it.   Their personalities are so different and unique.

We are very grateful for the relationships we have with our grandchildren. We pursued our grandchildren when they were very young. When we were babysitting, we would play blocks, read to them, and tell them stories. Perhaps the most fun was playing dolls and trucks with them - in other words, we enjoyed playing games that would excite their imaginations. Their little world was a fun place to be.

In a closet in our family room, we set up a playhouse. It accommodated a sink, refrigerator, stove with pots and pans, dishes and silverware, and a crib complete with a blanket. It was just large enough for a little three or four year old to play in and for Dottie to participate with them. Many tea parties and dinner parties were created in that little room. Playing house was a favorite game, even the little boys loved to join in. MomMom also had an old trunk full of dress-up clothes for both the boys and girls. How the grandchildren loved to dress up. When the little boys would get bored with all the girlie play and wanted more action, out came the trucks, boy-powered of course, complete with little boy noises, zooming all around the family room. The evening would

Kevin and Grant take a break from dress-ups to enjoy a story with PopPop.

end with a story, a glass of milk, a cracker and a cuddle, while we waited for Mom and Dad.

When the children outgrew the closet, we cleaned out an old tool shed and moved the playhouse furniture into it. The shed was ideally set among a few trees and soon proved to be the main attraction. It evolved into an imaginary world where the children made up all kinds of games. A favorite one was "Fox and Bunnies." Mommy Bunny and Daddy Bunny lived in the playhouse with all their little bunnies. Out in the green forest was "Reddy the Fox." MomMom would be Reddy. What a noise when Reddy tried to catch a little bunny! Of course, she never did catch one. All the bunnies were 'too quick' for Reddy.

In our backyard were three big climbing trees. The imagination of the little boys turned those trees into three ships, one being a pirate ship. One boy would climb to the top branches as the look-out scout. The others sailed the ship and hauled the sails. When the scout discovered an approaching ship, the three would climb aboard and capture the booty. Lunch time was always late that day.

While on lunch break, PopPop plays a game with granddaughter Julie.

Our relationship with our grandchildren deepened through the years when we started to have *special time* with each of our grandchildren. Every year, each grandchild would spend the night at our house around 37

Snuggle time with Ben, Matt, and Kristie.

the time of his or her birthday. It was that grandchild's turn to choose an activity – to do anything he or she wanted with us.

One of our many memories is of Jeff at four years old. A fox hunt was his adventure of choice, and into the woods we went, determined to catch that fox. Jeff sported a backpack with a plastic bat sticking out. In an effort to slay his fox, he was going to use the bat to hit the fox on the head, and then put him in his backpack. He was a determined hunter that day. With video camera in hand, I followed Jeff and Dottie through the woods. Jeff talked all the while looking for a fox to catch. Somehow the fox always eluded us. What a sad little boy when he came home with his empty sack.

Another *special time* was when Kristie and MomMom each took their baby dolls out to lunch in a nearby restaurant, sat them individually in high chairs and fed them part of their sandwiches. Although six-year-old Kristie received a lot of attention she never winked a eye. She changed the diaper without a blink, continuing to hold a conversation with MomMom while they were eating. She was a mommy and her baby came first. MomMom played right along with her.

On another occasion, Julie wanted to play school. She turned our bedroom into a school room. Of course, she was the teacher, and she proceeded to teach math. If MomMom did not behave, she would stand her in the corner and make her write on the black board, "*I will listen to my teacher.*" Chattering the whole time, she kept MomMom in line. Today Julie is a preschool teacher.

Trapping a bear is what Matthew at age eight had in mind for one of his *special times*. It was winter and he thought he could track a bear through the snow. We tramped through the

MomMom got bopped on the head with a snowball!

The explorers: Kristie, Amy, Andy Jeff, and Matt.

woods, looking for bear pawprints. Digging a big hole in the snow and laying broken tree branches over it, we built a bear trap. Afterwards we ended up at our neighbor's home for hot chocolate and cookies while we told our bear story. Early the next day we examined the trap. It was empty. However, this little boy never lost hope that one day he would trap a bear.

Amy at age seven had a doll named Samantha. At *special time* we always would have a tea party together that she loved to set up with our dolls. Of course, 'Lady Jane' was invited. Sewing was another interest for Amy. Dottie introduced her to sewing by making dresses for her doll.

It was apparent around the age of seven that Ben was our thinker. He would wake up in the morning with something big on his mind. One morning he woke up and all he wanted to talk about was the planets. He was fascinated with the universe. We always learned so much from him and loved his inquisitive little mind. He kept us on our toes.

Still in the game! PopPop, Ben, MomMom, Matt, and Jeff

Andy was our man of action. He liked the go carts and miniature golf, and he often beat us golf course! Playing basketball, football, baseball (really anything with a ball), was his love. There was a basketball court nearby, and MomMom would often play one-on-one with each of the grandsons until they were 13 or 14. We even had our own tournament rules.

The six younger grand children still continue to enjoy their special time. However, four of them Kevin, Grant Timothy and Lianna for about 15 years lived 3 hours away. During those years of visiting as often as we could we also appreciated their unselfishness in packing up their family of six and driving up for all the major holidays. In addition to visiting and special time, many precious pictures, homemade cars and reassured artwork have been thoughtfully sent and proudly displayed on the refrigerator, then

You win, Andy! How about another round?

later set aside for a scrap book. The mutual effort of staying in touch has been priceless.

Melanie and Stephen live nearby. They are both ten years old. *Special time* is still very much a part of their lives. Stephen is still a fan of Spider Man, a great chess player, and loves playing basketball. Melanie is active in soccer, plays the piano and violin. She also loves to play games. She is our family champion at Uno.

In the woods near our home we built a tepee from tree branches in the woods, and every *special time* the children want to see if it is still there. Believing that we are pioneers and that the Indians are watching us, we trudge through the woods. We end our day by walking back in the creek with our dirty old sneakers and pants rolled up to our knees. Many more stories could still be told, but we have tried to capture the idea of *special time* and how important it is to us to develop a relationship with each grandchild.

41

At the writing of this book, our youngest daughter Lisa, and her family have just settled near us. The grandchildren have not wasted any time catching up with *special time*. The four youngest cousins see each other often and have sleepovers, still

loving the dress-ups and adventures in the woods. We are grateful to have them nearby.

Having our grandchildren know us is important as well. We have shared with them our love story, how we met, fell in love, and married each other. Growing up, our daughters loved to hear their father tell the

'Special time' with Lianna and Melanie.

story. Now PopPop tells it like this:

"I met MomMom when she was 14 years old and I was 17, but she was too young to date. It was a rainy Sunday night. Our two youth groups were meeting at my church, and her Youth Group was late so we started the program without them. I was sitting on the end of a row of chairs against the back wall right next to the door. Suddenly the door opened, and MomMom's face came around the corner asking if this was the right church. Her face was so close and she was so beautiful. I could only stammer 'Yes!' as she quickly disappeared. Wow! Who was that?! I was stunned. When she returned with the rest of the group, I couldn't keep my eyes off her all evening. I was smitten! I had to wait four years for her to grow up. When MomMom turned 18 we started dating, and one year later, after I

42

graduated from college, I asked her to marry me. We have loved each other ever since."

The story would end with a kiss and a hug. To this day the grandchildren love to hear it again and again, and we love to tell it.

As the grandchildren have grown older, our relationships have only deepened. The younger ones still love our times in the woods, basketball, swimming, storytime and, of course, *special time*. What is changing is our relationship with our young-adult grandchildren. We are now reaping the many blessings from all of the early years of sowing into their lives, playing games, telling stories and *special time*.

There is nothing more exciting for us than a teenage grandchild stopping in for a chat, which often provided us with information on how to pray for them; i.e., their spiritual life, their college decisions, work plans, and their future spouses.

A generational 'rap' with Matt and Ben.

There is no greater joy as grandparents than to be involved in our grandchildren's lives with the time they have made available to us.

With our teenage grandchildren, we are learning the value of waiting to speak into their lives and continuing to build trust in our relationships. Most of the time we are more like a sounding board; everyone needs someone to listen to them. By just listening, our grandchildren will often solve their own problems. Wherever the conversation goes, we always direct the grandchild to talk with his parents about any given situation. We are not accountable for their upbringing;

that is their parents' responsibility. As grandparents, it is our commitment to inform the parents about any conversation we might have had with their children. The grandchildren know that we do not keep secrets from their parents. We do not want the parents to feel threatened by our relationship with their children. This guideline has enabled us to preserve our relationship with our own children.

Over the years the Lord has let us build a trust in our grandchildren's lives. He has let us see into their young hearts with His compassion and understanding. If there is any wisdom to be learned, we are still learning. When the Lord opens a window into the heart of one of our grandchildren, we try to remember it is a privilege and that we are not to 'rearrange the furniture.' We pray for them, listen to their hearts, observe where the 'furniture' is placed, and only make suggestions. Since the window of the heart is only open for so long, we thank the Lord for that opportunity. Directing them to their parents and pointing them to the Lord is the best practice for that special moment.

This September, 2008, we will be celebrating our 50th wedding anniversary. Our hearts are overflowing with thanksgiving to the Lord for the special friendship we share with each of our children and grandchildren. Truly we can say, *"The generation of the upright will be blessed." (Psalm 112:2 ESV)*

Mt. Washington, here we come!

Entering the Window of a Young Heart

"I will open my mouth in parables, I will utter hidden things, things from of old - what we have heard and known, what our fathers have told us."

Psalm 78:2, 3 NIV

Over the years we have had many opportunities to walk alongside our children as they have imparted wisdom to our growing brood of grandchildren. What a joyful privilege this has been; and what a challenge as well! The challenge has been to offer counsel in such a way that the grandchildren can understand and apply it to their own lives. As we sought the Lord for guidance ourselves, we sensed His answer to us was to tell them stories.

As a result, storytelling has indeed become one of our greatest pleasures and one of the most effective endeavors we have experienced as grandparents in helping our grandchildren to apply godly wisdom to their lives. The Lord has yielded fruit in the hearts of our grandchildren. Purposeful stories have been a subtle yet powerful teaching tool in MomMom's creative tool box. As grandparents, we have used storytelling successfully to reach the hearts of our grandchildren and to help them apply wisdom to their own lives. Here is how it works.

Dottie creates an imaginary story that can illustrate a moral lesson. She gets her ideas after talking to one of our daughters about a specific character issue they have been working on with one of their children. For instance, jealousy, lying, or stealing could be a current topic.

Dottie has a family of characters. They can either be animals or people, but the stories are short and to-the-point. When the children are about 2 - 4 years old, animal stories are their favorites. Later, around the age of five or six years, Dottie tell stories about an imaginary little boy named George and his friend Jennifer. These tales became *The Adventures of George and Jennifer.* The children never know how old George and Jennifer really are and they never ask. They just assume that George and Jennifer are their own present age. Dottie is still making up stories today for the five youngest grandchildren.

Tell me a story, MomMom!

One of her earliest stories was created when our grandson Jeff was a baby. As jealousy blossomed in a 2 ½ year old sister's heart, it became apparent that we had a moral issue at hand. Coming alongside the parents, Dottie lent her creative support. She took the big sister aside and proceeded to ask her gentle, purposeful questions. *"Do you know what jealousy is, Honey?"* Mom Mom probed. At 2 ½ years old, the door was opened for a good story…

46

"Fluffy was a cute little bunny who lived in the Green Forest with her Mommy and Daddy. For years it had been just the three of them: Mommy Bunny, Daddy Bunny and Fluffy. Fluffy liked it that way. She had Mommy and Daddy all to herself. One day, her mommy brought home a baby brother bunny. And how do you think Fluffy felt about that?"

Now she had her granddaughter's rapt attention. Dottie transitioned into her lesson using Fluffy as the object of instruction. Dottie was able to share what jealousy looked like.

"You see, Fluffy was jealous because she was afraid that her new little brother bunny would take all of Mommy's and Daddy's time and attention away from her. She thought Mommy and Daddy would love the new baby bunny more than they loved her. Fluffy did not like the baby bunny and pouted in a corner.

Mommy and Daddy saw their little Fluffy's sad face and assured Fluffy that they had a very special love in their hearts just for her. Fluffy thought to herself, 'I am so much bigger than the baby bunny. I don't think I want to be a baby and wear diapers anymore. I want to be a big helper.' That was a big decision for Fluffy to make.

That night, Fluffy prayed and asked the God-who-makes-little-bunnies to forgive her for being jealous of her new baby bunny brother. She later thanked the God-who-makes-little-bunnies for her new little brother bunny. Then she lay awake for awhile wondering how she could become the best big sister bunny."

Our granddaughter shifted in her seat and moved a little closer as MomMom continued, *"In the morning, after she awoke and dressed herself, Fluffy went downstairs and asked her mommy how she could help take care of the baby bunny today.*

47

Mommy was so happy to have a big bunny to help her! Fluffy had learned that nothing would ever stop her mommy and daddy from loving her!"

Still cuddling together, MomMom began to draw out our little granddaughter with thoughtful and intentional questions: *"Are you afraid your baby brother might take Mommy and Daddy's attention away from you? Do you know that God has a very special plan for your life when He sent you to Mommy and Daddy first so you could become a helpful big sister? Do you think perhaps God sent your baby brother to become your special friend as you grow up?"*

Dottie concluded with a lesson that imparted wisdom to our granddaughter and helped apply that wisdom to her own life: God sent the perfect baby brother just for her, He has a special plan for her, and has placed her perfectly in her family; no one can ever take her place.

Some of Dottie's stories have provoked our granddaughters to imitate the imaginary characters themselves. We had one granddaughter who would often listen to a story, go home, and act it out. When this granddaughter was seven years old, Dottie wanted the grandchildren to know that Halloween was not a holiday to celebrate. The parents were in agreement and grateful to have Dottie help them out.

Knowing how children like Halloween dress-up, candy, and parties, MomMom told a story to our first grandchild about how George and Jennifer turned a neighborhood Halloween party into a neighborhood Hallelujah Party. We were amazed and delighted when Julie re-enacted the story, word-for-word, in her neighborhood. She sent out invitations inviting her friends. Dressed up as Bible characters, her guests played games and received prizes for the most authentic costumes. Tracts that shared the gospel were given to all who attended. The children loved the Hallelujah Party and wanted one the following year.

By acting out a godly alternative through storytelling, Dottie had subtly and effectively imparted a lesson.

Not all of our stories have been make-believe. Sometimes the true stories have been far more memorable than anything we could create in our imaginations. Roger loves to tell the story to our open-mouthed grandchildren of the time he evaded death as an impulsive 13 year old one cold winter day. His buddies and he gathered at a river to ice skate. They chose to skate at an idle backwater river with thick ice. Without thinking or testing the ice for safety, he left the thick ice and skated across the thinner ice covering the flowing river as the ice cracked behind him. All he could think of was that he had to skate back over the same ice - and he proceeded to do it! The Lord must have sent an angel to guard him that day, because he shouldn't really be alive today to tell this story since Julie, Ben, Jeff, Matt, Amy, Kristie, Andy, Kevin, Grant, Timmy, Melanie, Stephen and Lianna would not

be here today if God had not shown mercy to such a foolish young man. They look at him with wonder as he exhorts them by saying, *"Don't you ever be as foolish as your PopPop!"*

As grandparents, we have collected an arsenal of stories over the years, and they are often about our own experiences in life. Our grandchildren especially love to hear flashback memories about their mothers when they were little girls. Dottie started putting her stories on cassette. Perhaps one day we will publish *The Adventures of George and Jennifer* for each of our grandchildren to share with our great-grandchildren. What a rich blessing that would be!

49

Whether our stories are true or imaginary, it has been a great means of bonding with our grandchildren and a fruitful investment to help shape their hearts. We see these stories as footprints that we are leaving behind for another generation.

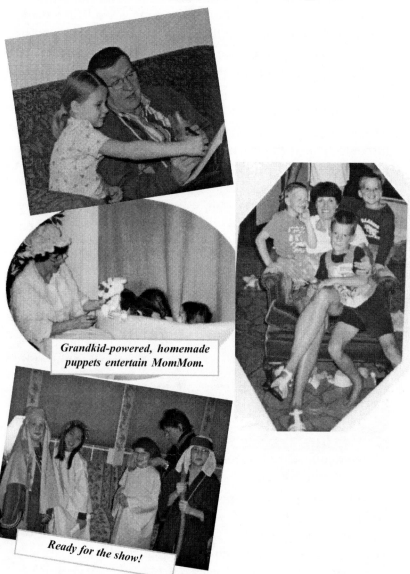

Grandkid-powered, homemade puppets entertain MomMom.

Ready for the show!

Making Memories

"The memory of the righteous is a blessing..."
Proverbs 10:7 ESV

"When your children ask in time to come, 'what do those stones mean to you?' then you shall tell them that the waters of the Jordan were cut off before the ark of the covenant of the LORD. When it passed over the Jordan, the waters of the Jordan were cut off. So these stones shall be to the people of Israel 'a memorial forever.'"
Joshua 4:6, 7 ESV

In the Old Testament, we see how the Lord instructed His people to build memorials to remember His deeds from generation to generation. Memories are important. Year after year our grandchildren look forward to certain times with great expectation as kinship-uniting events.

In our experience, children love family traditions. It seems to give them a sense of security and being 'in the know' about what is going to happen year after year. Our young families

51

are very busy with everyday activities. As an extended family, we try to all meet at least every three months. Not only is it essential for the cousins to grow up together and be good friends, but it is important to the adults to have that time together as well. We usually will meet at our home. Yes, it is wall-to-wall children, but it is MomMom's and PopPop's house. All the grandchildren know where the cookie jar is and the closet of toys.

We'd like to describe for you some of the traditions we have established in our family to give you some ideas of the things you can do. Of course, your own traditions will look different than ours and will be as unique as your family. The important thing is to establish traditions that will strengthen and encourage your family and honor the Lord as 'a memorial forever.' (Joshua 4:7)

Our Family Christmas Tradition

One of our favorite family traditions is at Christmas when we celebrate as a family the birth of our Lord Jesus Christ. We have made the suggestion that each daughter celebrates first with her own family to make their own traditions before gathering at our home. Later when we gather at our home, the first thing we do is to honor the Lord by reenacting the Christmas pageant. MomMom dresses each of the grandchildren from 12 years old and younger in costumes. Between the doorway to our sun porch

and living room MomMom hangs up a curtain. PopPop sits on the side and reads the Christmas story. Each scene is acted out by the grandchildren and carols are sung. If

PopPop narrates the Christmas story.

there is a real baby available, he/she will appear in the manger. For the past 15 years we've been able to continue this tradition.

As the family has grown, we have had to re-assess our family Christmas. Our new great-granddaughter was the baby Jesus this year. It was a delight to have a baby in the family again. With two more engaged couples in the family, we are slowly outgrowing our home.

Change has been a difficult word for us as we've grown older. Kindly, God leads us back to our knees, confessing our selfish desires to keep Christmas the same. We are realizing that it is time for us to step back again and let the next generation come forth. Our children are now the

Steven was the herald for our family's 15th annual Christmas pageant.

grandparents and they will be serving their children in the grandparent's role. We soon may have to divide into three Christmas celebrations with Dottie and I attending each separate one. We will have to wait on the Lord to lead us.

The Family Blessing

A new tradition that we started a few years ago began in one of our daughter's families and has spread to the extended family. We call it the 'family blessing.' Usually it is expressed on a birthday, graduation, or Father's or Mother's Day celebration. After dinner, we sit around the table to honor a special family member by having each one present - even the little ones - share a word of encouragement or appreciation about the one being honored.

Recently on Mother's Day, it was our oldest daughter and her family's turn to come for dinner to celebrate with us.

Our son-in-law did a very gracious thing. He had the idea of blessing all three mothers present that day: our daughter, Dottie, and Dottie's mother who was living with us at the time. What joy it was to sit and listen to the grandchildren honor their mother and hear the affect she has had on their lives. Being homeschooled children, each one expressed his or her gratitude for her teaching, care, and patience.   Affectionate and grateful words were expressed by her husband. Both of us participated as well.

Then it was Dottie's turn. It was a humbling experience to hear the expressions of love from each of the grandchildren, our daughter, our son-in-law, and ending with myself. Dottie's heart was deeply moved and very much aware that the blessing is only the continuing work of God's grace in her life.

Dottie's mom was last. Imagine her delight as five of her great-grandchildren, her granddaughter and her husband, and her daughter and her son-in-law participated in honoring her. Proverbs 31:30 was taking place in our home as the children blessed their mothers.

Our Family Easter Tradition

Our family Easter celebration is a day to remember. As a family, we celebrate on the Saturday before Easter. This allows our daughters to enjoy Easter with their in-laws.

When our family gathers together, our first desire is to honor the Lord. It is His Resurrection Day. On one Easter our older grandchildren set up a foot washing service for the family. What a blessed cleansing it was. Durint the ceremony we discussed how Jesus, God's only Son, came to earth as a baby, lived among us, died, rose again and ascended to the right hand of the Father is a reminder that we all need to hear. Needless to say this was a most memorable experience.

Ever since the grandchildren were young, the candy scramblehas been an awaited event. Candy is hidden in three areas of our home, including downstairs in the finished basement.

Additionally, an individual small gift is wrapped and hidden for each child. Baskets are given out for each child - even the teenagers - to gather their treasures. We make those anxious teenagers wait for the younger children to finish first before they are allowed the mad dash down the stairs to scavenge the basement. In less than ten minutes, the baskets are full and gifts are found. When our oldest granddaughter was married, we thought she would want to stop participating, but she was right there with her basket ready to go. Chocolate kisses and jelly beans are

The hunt is on! Let's get Started!

apparently hard to resist even when you're an adult!

After dinner we celebrate the birthdays that have occurred in the past three months. Later in the evening, the girls help me clean up the dishes, pick up the toys in the basement and arrange the furniture. Then it is time to go home. Hugs are given and memories are again stored away for another year. It is a delightful yet exhausting day for two aging grandparents now ready to 'hit the sack.'

The Wood Fairies Tradition

As long as she can remember, Dottie and her two brothers would spend a week with their grandparents in New Hampshire. Not long after Dottie and I were married, the summer-home became the property of her parents. Every summer we would

spend two weeks at 'camp' with Dottie's parents, affectionately known as 'Mucky' and 'Gamu.'

Gamu started the tradition of the wood fairies at camp when the girls were young. She told the story of how the wood fairies loved children. Every night when the children were asleep, the fairies would come out of their houses and fly around the woods looking for places to hide their treasure for the children. The treasure was usually a small plastic ring, penny candy, or a small toy. In the morning, the children knew the signal: when the kitchen curtains were flung open at Gamu's camp, it was time to start the hunt. Before the children were awake, Gamu would go out in the woods with a ball of cotton. She would put small pieces of it on different bushes, rocks and grasses that led to the 'treasure hideout.' What excitement! This went on for

years. When the two older girls learned the secret, they kept it from their younger sister. Pretty soon, they all had it figured out and just wanted the toys!

Look what the fairies left!

In the summer of 1983, our first grandchild arrived. Within the next five years, five more grandchildren were born with more on the way. Because the cousins were so close in age, they were very good buddies and wanted to be together. We started to vacation in New Hampshire again, only now we were the grandparents!

Yes, the family tradition of the wood fairies continues, though with a little variation. With so many grandchildren, candy soon replaced the plastic toys. It was now MomMom's turn to play the fairy and leave the treats. One year the chipmunks found the candy first and only the wrappers were left! The next night before the children went to bed, they wrote a note to the wood fairies saying, "Please hide the candy in a safer spot with better wrappers." As the older children learned about the fairies, it was fun for them to participate, plus they made the fairies more believable for the younger ones.

We have videos of the children following the fluffy white cotton trail of the fairies, and the wonderful look of surprise on their faces when they first find the candy. The wood fairy is a family tradition that will never be forgotten and will probably continue into the next generation.

Tradition of Swimming to the Island

Another tradition at camp that began when the girls were young was the swim to the island. The camp sits beside the shore of a 50 acre lake with a very small island in the middle about a quarter of a mile away. Any child at least ten years old was allowed the choice to swim to the island. We would all gather at the shore of the lake and set out. Since we made the swim into such a big deal to all of us, an observer may have thought we were swimming the English Channel!

We always had a rowboat and canoe available for the swimmers to grab on to if they felt the need. While the island

Look who's king of the mountain!

I'll save you!

57

wasn't that large, it could be explored on foot, and at the same time allow the grandchildren time to catch their breath before the return swim. Each child regarded his first time to the island and back as a milestone to be remembered, whether he finished in the water or in a canoe.

A trip to the ice cream store was next. Though it was a hefty two-mile hike, the reward of an ice cream cone motivated them to quickly became accomplished swimmers!

Climbing Mt. Washington - The Highlight of the Week

Any grandchild who was at least ten years old could participate in the annual climb up Mt. Washington. This trip was an opportunity to impress upon everyone the awesomeness of God's creation. Everything about Mt. Washington was a wonder. Starting at Pinkham Notch Ranger Station, we would hike the Tuckerman Ravine Trail. It was a challenge to keep the younger and more energetic children from running ahead. Stopping to appreciate the wonders of God would come years later. For the moment, their little legs would run off to the first waterfall before they took their first breath. By the time we would catch up with them, they had raced through the quiet forest, crossed a thrashing brook, and were waiting for us with their boots off and soaking their feet in the cool mountain stream. Little did they know that they needed to reserve their energy for what lay ahead.

We would then begin the rugged ascent. Surrounded on three sides with steep rocky walls, Tuckerman's Ravine gave the feeling to us of being in the Alps. At this point, all the family gathered together to start the big push up the headwall.

For the second half of our climb, the younger grandchildren stayed closer to us. The trail begins by paralleling a rushing mountain stream which pours down the rocky side of the canyon. At this point, although it was August, snow is still in the canyon. The steep wall becomes stones arranged as steps.

Reaching the headwall, we are met with whipping winds as we cling to the mountain. Sweaters, jackets and hats are donned for the chilling final stretch called 'the cone.' It requires agility to jump from one boulder to the next. If the clouds close in, the yellow paint on the rocks mark the trail. The higher we climb, the air gets thinner making it harder to breathe even for the little

We made it!
Top of Mt. Washington

ones. Urged on by the steam whistle of the Cog Railway as it leaves the station, the summit is now in sight. At last, we have a chance to rest, look around, and explore. It was often cold and windy at the top, but that never deterred any of us from enjoying the spectacular display of God's beauty.

On the return trip, although not as breathless as the ascent, we found it every bit as rugged on our legs. We would finish our hike, returning by nightfall, load into the van, and head back to camp. Everyone felt that they had experienced a real adventure, and the newer hikers were proud to claim another real achievement in their life with the family.

Later as the leadership began to pass to the sons-in-law, a bi-annual four-day hike for the men of the family was initiated. Grandsons, beginning at 13 years of age, could join the men in hiking the Appalachian

Camping in the rain is fun, too!

59

Trail, whitewater canoeing on the Delaware River, or hiking the mountains of the West. Each year was different and required

overnight stays on the trail or river bank. Fortunately, Roger is still able to participate, although the mountains seem to get higher each year. This past August the Lord blessed him with a five-day hike in

The guys at Glacier National Park.

Glacier National Park with five grandsons and three sons-in-law. But that is another story.

With our family maturing, we have had to make some major adjustments. The camp in New England is too far away for the grandchildren who have to work in the summers, so now

we have started a new tradition. Roger is able to rent a large enough place for the entire family (which now includes new brides and a great grandchild) to be together. It is close enough for the grandchildren who have to work to be with us on the weekends. There is hiking, swimming, tennis, volleyball, and miniature golf available, plus plenty of rest for mom and dad, MomMom and PopPop. For our four

Taking a hiking break with Timmy.

Family volleyball - PopPop takes a rest.

youngest grandchildren and our great granddaughter, it is 'seventh heaven'! They have started their own memories.

When repeated year after year, these traditions remind us of God's kindness to make us a family. Because the young children are so familiar with these customs, it allows them to assume a measure of leadership as they confidently know what is going to happen each year that we repeat the tradition.

We have our walking sticks ready to go!

As we grow older, the memories of these times with our grandchildren are a blessing. They are special treasures hidden in our hearts that we often reflect upon as we sit on the deck enjoying the gentle evening breeze. The years of grandparenting will someday come to an end. Until then our grandchildren are prayerfully in our hearts as they raise their families and allow us to making memories with them.

The four camp cooks.

Hamburgers and hotdogs for dinner back at

Grandchildren's Comments

"I will sing of the steadfast love of the LORD, forever; with my mouth I will make known your faithfulness to all generations."
Psalm 89:1 ESV

"Unless the LORD builds the house, those who build it labor in vain...Behold, children are a heritage from the LORD, the fruit of the womb a reward." Psalm 127:1, 3 ESV

When our girls were young, we were aware of how much our marriage meant to them. Anytime we had a disagreement the girls were right there trying to distract us to make us happy. We had to learn to keep our disagreements behind closed doors or out on a walk; little eyes were watching. We realized later that our making up did not necessarily mean that the girls understood that we had made up. We had to tell them that Mommy and Daddy loved each other and everything would be all right. To hear or to see us arguing or disrespecting each other threatened their security. We were their whole world. It was the way God designed it.

Our marriage relationship has grown over the last 50 years by the grace of God. His Word has been to us a continuous unveiling of how to walk in our relationship as demonstrated by Christ and His bride. We are still learning to walk this walk. Over the years, the Lord has blessed us with biblical sermons, teaching seminars, books, friends, and our married children. They have all contributed to who we are today.

When writing this book we thought that it would be interesting to see how our grandchildren felt about our marriage and if it was important to them. To help answer this question we sent out e-mails to our thirteen grandchildren and asked them these questions:

- "Is it important to you that we are still married today and why?"
- "What effect has our marriage had upon you?"

As grandparents we had no idea how much they have been watching and listening. It was an eye-opener. The following are their responses:

JULIE (24 years old)

"One of the things that I love about your marriage is how 'in love' PopPop is with MomMom. Growing up, my mom would always tell us stories about how MomMom would wear curlers in her hair and PopPop would always say, 'Mommy's such a pretty mommy!' The fact that he still says that when we're around is such a blessing. It is a great example to your grandkids of what a godly, loving, fun marriage looks like.

The fact that MomMom adores PopPop and treasures his wisdom is a great legacy for what submission should look like. MomMom didn't just begrudgingly go about with the budget envelope, but esteemed PopPop's wisdom for putting them on a budget that way. I remember MomMom taking money out of her envelopes when we would be shopping and sharing with me how PopPop was so wise and generous with money. MomMom never grumbled about her budget.

It's great to hear the stories about how PopPop lead the family through transitional job times and about how Mom-Mom always supported PopPop and made ends meet. PopPop has always been the provider, but MomMom has always been the joyful helper…whether that meant sewing Bible covers or helping him teach kids God's way.

When I think of 'growing old' with my husband, you folks come to mind. The fact that you are still each other's best friend gives me vision for the future of what I want to build with Jake. I've heard stories from your younger years from my mom and my aunts, and I've seen with my own eyes what your love looks like now. I know that you have only grown more in love over time. As MomMom says, you guys are 'so much part of each other that it would be difficult to tell who is who.' I want to build that kind of intimate friendship with Jake, and your example is the best I know!"

BEN (23 years old)

"Your marriage relationship has affected me in ways that I can't begin to describe. In complete honesty, I find myself taking it for granted many times, as I also do with my own parent's marriage. However, when looking deeply into it, it

DOES matter a lot that you've stayed together as a couple. First, it gives me an opportunity to have my eyes opened by the Lord to see that it's His grace behind your growing together and staying together in your marriage. Second, I know I'll desire to put into practice what I've observed from you in your example, all for His glory.

Your example has been incredible in showing me what a marriage looks like in the everyday life scenario. I have been watching and listening over the years and I have to say, it's one thing to talk well about something; it's another thing to put things into practice. You are a model of what a long-lasting marriage looks like, rooted in the Gospel. You encourage me for my marriage. I, too, by the grace of God will be a faithful husband and provider."

JEFF (22 years old)

"I don't want to miss the opportunity to let you know how much your marriage has affected me. First, it causes me to anticipate my own marriage. Many of my friends have expressed fear about getting married, because they have seen so many bad marriages. However, this is not the case for me. Seeing you guys in love after all those years, makes me long for that kind of companionship for myself.

Second, your marriage encourages my faith in God. Not only have you been married for a long time, but your marriage is still vibrant. I know that this is because of the grace of God on both of your lives. Seeing how God blesses those couples who place their trust in Him, gives me faith that my future marriage will also be a success in Him.

Third, the wisdom that you pass down about marriage is invaluable. The testimony of your marriage makes me want to learn as much as I can from you about how to have a godly marriage. I will never forget a conversation I had with MomMom about taking an interest in your spouse's interests. Marriage is not all about me! You emphasized the necessity of living one harmonious life together by keeping short accounts and forgiving each other daily. I remember even my great grandmother Gamu who told me to always make time for your spouse, no matter what. Coming from a woman who was married for 64 years, I think I should pay attention to what she says!"

MATTHEW (21 years old)

"In response to your questions, I think it is very important that you and PopPop are still married. I see how much my Mom is influenced positively by your relationship together, and how many of the things that you have instilled in her heart have come into my home as well and influenced us kids. My parents' marriage is affected by your marriage as well, in a sense that my Mom has found a man that is similar to her father in many ways. They are both kind, caring, and gentle.

Your marriage also says a lot about your personalities and convictions. I think it is amazing that you guys are still fully involved in one another's lives after being married for so long. It is sad for me to hear some of the ambulance personnel that I ride with just complain and talk down on their marriages, and they are much younger than you guys. If your marriage ever broke down, I couldn't talk about my holiday experiences at your house positively. My head would go around in a million circles and I honestly wouldn't know how to handle it. Even though it wouldn't be my parents, you two are still my parents in a sense that you have raised my Mom and influenced my parents in their marriage. My Mom loves you both so much and especially loves 'girl talks' with you, MomMom, and it would affect her greatly to see her parents separated and I know it would take its toll at my house, too.

Your marriage means everything to me, and is an example of what I strive to be when I'm your age. I am sure there have been countless trials you've faced together in your marriage. The way I have seen you live your lives is an example that I will always be affected by. When my mother had breast cancer, you were on your knees for both Mom and Dad. Your prayers and support meant a lot to me and my whole family. There is no hesitation in my mind when I think about how much your marriage has influenced my life in only a positive manner. By the grace of God I desire to be like you. I want to care for my wife someday in the exact way that PopPop cares for you, MomMom. He loves you more than himself and I know only the Lord enables him to do so."

AMY (20 years old)

"When you asked me how your marriage has affected me, the first thing that popped into my head was that it gives me faith for the future. Not only do I have the privilege of observing my parents, but in watching you guys I have seen what a godly marriage should look like!!! It is so evident that you both treasure and respect one anther deeply, and that really is an encouragement and example to me. I know that the reason you two keep growing in your love for one another is because you have centered your marriage around the gospel. Your example of keeping Christ first in all things has obviously had a profound impact on your marriage. I so enjoy watching the way you guys express your love for each other, and I pray that I can emulate your example. I trust that in following your example, God is going to bless me with a wonderful marriage that only gets better every year. So thank you for your example…it gives me such faith for my marriage and future."

KRISTIE (18 years old)

"Your marriage is so important to me, because you give us an example to look up to as the 'head' of our family as grandparents. As you both follow Christ's will for your life together as a couple, you give reassurance to both my parents and your grandchildren for us to follow and admire. I have never once questioned your love for each other, which is incredible in the day that we live in. Even the simplest thing, like holding each other's hands, gave me the reassurance that you two would never leave each other, and it always got rid of any fears that I could have had.

Also, I've always appreciated how much you have striven to first direct us to our parents in any personal situation. There have been many times that we kids have come to you with what's going on in our lives, and you've always come alongside our parents and have never opposed what they were saying. If you

69

would have, I would have only questioned even more what they were saying, but you always helped us to desire to please our parents. You've helped me to see that as I honor them, I ultimately honor God Himself.

Lastly, you have always looked for ways to spend time with us and get to know us more. I've had so many memories throughout my life that include you both, and it's actually some of those memories that stick with me most. It was always a huge deal when you would seek me out, and because of the relationship you have developed with me throughout my childhood, we can now enjoy such a deep relationship. I want you around for my children, so please take care of your health. I am praying for you guys."

ANDY (17 years old)
"I think that your marriage has been one of the greatest examples I know of walking together in godliness. I have been able to see what a godly marriage looks like after fifty years. Your marriage has given me a perspective on how to love one person for a lifetime. Your affections for each other have been clearly demonstrated every time I have seen you. It is clear that you two are not bored of each other and I thank God for that! Marriage is far from my mind now, but I have you guys and my parents to thank for a great example.

You have loved every single grandchild with great affection. You have always tried to orchestrate your lives around our interests and have striven to know each one individually. Your dedication to family has affected my life to centralize my life around my family, and it has been your example to do this."

KEVIN (15 years old)

"Your marriage is a godly example for me to draw from. Your marriage helps keep the family together. What I like most is that you have been together a long time. I am thankful that I have grandparents who still love each other and can show their affections.

I have great memories of playing with you guys; the fairy hunts in the woods, holidays at your home, 'special time' (mini golf, etc.), being snowed-in with you when Mom and Dad went away for a weekend together, hikes in the woods, and playing ball in the park.

Every time we were together I can tell that you like each other and enjoy being together whether it is with us kids or just yourselves. I am grateful that our family moved to be near you."

GRANT (14 years old)

"What I like the most is that you are still together and get along. You have a God-glorifying marriage. You care for and love each other. You do things for each other and others. You never speak harshly to each other.

You like to be with us. I can tell you love me and that you don't have a favorite grandchild. It is like having more parents in my life to have fun with, talk to, and who love me. You are a great example to my parents of a godly couple and for me with my future wife. I am glad that we have moved closer to you."

TIMOTHY (11 years old)

"I know that you would not be happy without each other. It would be harder to see you if you weren't married to each other. You wouldn't know each other very well. I can tell that you have a good marriage because you care for each other and have fun together. You like to be together and share. You can help me learn more about marriage when I am older. I like living near you now. I love to play in the woods together and walk the creek and keep the tepee repaired"

MELANIE (10 years old)

"You make me happy in so many ways. You like to play enjoyable kinds of games with me. When I sleep over there, you even make a place beside your bed, so I can sleep with you. You both like taking me on walks in different parks where we can talk together. When I have special time with you MomMom, you tell me that I can do anything I want! I like that. PopPop, I like it when we watch Discovery Channel and you even let me hold the remote and change the channel, too. You tell me things I need to know about God and how important He is to you. I love you both with all my heart!"

STEPHEN (10 years old)

"I'm glad that you are married. It makes me feel happy that my parents and grandparents and my great grandparents were/are happily married. I'm glad that you raised my mom so well so that she could be a good mom to me. I'm glad that you are friends. I'm glad that you are wise and always help each other when you need to. I'm glad that we always have 'special time' when I become a year older and many other times."

LIANNA (9 years old)

"I'm glad you like each other. I like to come to your house. I like to play games with you. I like George and Jennifer stories. You have shown that God is kind and that He loves me too."

And last but not least, our first great grandchild offers this contribution:

MacKenzie (6 months old)
Gahgah...goo...<*blurp*>...bah bah ...mahmah...bbbbb!

Epilogue

It is our prayer that after you have read this book, you will have been encouraged to pursue your God-given gift to grandparent. We were not prefect grandparents, as you have read. We made plenty of mistakes, but we were the prefect grandparents for our thirteen grandchildren that the Lord gave to us. You also are the prefect grandparents for your grandchildren. The Lord has placed each of us in our families to play a particular role, and as we age, our calling changes. Whatever role the Lord calls upon us to play as grandparents, we know the Lord is able to equip us to impact the next generation with the Gospel. You have read our story. Your story can be an even better one. The Lord is faithful and, by the presence of the Holy Spirit in our lives, His grace is more than sufficient..

Addendum #1:   Sharing ideas

The following is a list of ideas that were shared at a night set aside for grandmothers at our daughter's church. How grateful we are that the Lord has sent such godly women to her church to help pave the way for this marvelous season of life! The ideas were so overflowing that she had a hard time writing them down; therefore, they are in no particular order.

PRACTICAL IDEAS:

1. UPROMISE.COM - Every time you use your credit card at certain stores or buy specific items, immediately a small percentage is deducted from the purchase price and put into this account set aside for your grandchild's future education.

2. Give savings bonds toward college for birthdays and Christmas in addition to gifts.

3. Buy special pajamas for them, once in the spring and once in the fall.

4. Bring along practical needs when visiting: diapers, formula, etc.

5. Save loose change and give it to your daughter.

FUN IDEAS:

1. Give a favorite book along with a tape of grandmother reading the story.

2. Create a tape of grandmother reading a bunch of different stories.

3. Create a personalized tape of grandmother singing songs using their names.

4. Tell made up stories and have them act them out.

5. Have them make up their own stories.

6. Have a special pet name for each grandchild.

7. Have talent shows with the children.

8. Find pictures of your daughter as she was growing up and tell about her life by adding silly stories.

9. Save all of the things that your grandchildren make and display them. They love to visit their creations and appreciate that you've found a special spot.

10. When a child moves up to being a toddler, have a ritual of buying a special quilt for them for being so big.

11. Make a photo album of each grandchild.

12. Take special pictures of a trip spent together and make a photo album to remember the time.

13. Make a photo album of all of their cousins and aunts and uncles.

14. Buy or make a personalized calendar.

15. Make a personalized puzzle (there are stores that do this).

16. Make them their own Christmas stocking to use every year. It will become an heirloom.

GRANDCHILDREN FAR AWAY:

1. Understand that it takes a while to connect.

2. Send packages every now and then - just because.

3. Send money to the child to take his or her mommy out.

4. Send money for the dollar store for them to buy gifts for siblings (birthdays).

5. Send cards with stickers or something special in them.

6. Remember to send Easter and Christmas cards; stick in some money too!

7. Invest in a webcam or "skype." It is great to see faces.

8. Mail books you get from yard sales. It's cheaper to send them as they go media mail.

FINAL TIPS FOR SUCCESSFUL GRAND PARENTING:

1. Give your grandchild your complete attention when you are with him/her.

2. Have individual dates with each grandchild.

3. Remember they are not your children, but you are a support to their parents.

4. They are a gift from the Lord and a blessing that you do not want to miss.

Addendum #2:
Grandma's Hand's
-Author Unknown

Counter-clockwise from top - 4 generations: MacKenzie, Julie, Kim, and MomMom.

Grandma, some ninety plus years, sat feeble on the patio bench. She didn't move, just sat with her head down staring at her hands. When I sat down beside her, she didn't acknowledge my presence, and the longer I sat I wondered if she was OK.

Finally, not really wanting to disturb her but wanting to check on her at the same time, I asked if she was OK. She raised her head and looked at me and smiled.

"Yes, I'm fine, thank you for asking," she said in a clear strong voice.

"I didn't mean to disturb you, Grandma, but you were just sitting here staring at your hands and I wanted to make sure you were OK," I explained to her.

"Have you ever looked at your hands?" she asked. "I mean, *really* looked at your hands?"

I slowly opened my hands and stared down at them. I turned them over, palms up and then palms down. No, I guess I had never really looked at my hands as I tried to figure out the point she was making. Grandma smiled and related this story:

"Stop and think for a moment about the hands you have, how they have served you well throughout your years. These hands, though wrinkled, shriveled and weak have been the tools I have used all my life to reach out and grab and embrace life. They braced and caught my fall when as a toddler I crashed upon the floor. They put food in my mouth and clothes on my back. As a child, my mother taught me to fold them in prayer.

They tied my shoes and pulled on my boots. They dried the tears of my children and caressed the love of my life. They wiped my tears when my husband went off to war. They have been dirty, scraped and raw, swollen and bent. They were uneasy and clumsy when I tried to hold our newborn daughter.

Decorated with my wedding band they showed the world that I was married and loved someone special! They wrote the letters home and trembled and shook when I buried my parents and spouse. They have held children and grand children, consoled neighbors, and shook in fists of anger when I didn't understand.

They have covered my face, combed my hair, and washed and cleansed the rest of my body. They have been sticky and wet, bent and broken, dried and raw. And to this day when not much of anything else of me works real well these hands hold me up, lay me down, and again continue to fold in prayer.

These hands are the mark of where I've been and the ruggedness of life. But more importantly it will be these hands that God will reach out and take when he leads me home. And with my hands He will lift me to His side and there I will use these hands to touch the face of Christ."

I will never look at my hands the same again. But I remember God reached out and took my grandma's hands and led her home.

When my hands are hurt or sore or when I stroke the face of my children and husband I think of grandma. I know she has been stroked and caressed and held by the hands of God. I too want to touch the face of God and feel His hands upon my face. 79